# Hinds' Feet on High Places

## by
## Hannah Hurnard

*Arranged by Dian Layton*

*Illustrated by JoAnn Edington*

**Destiny Image® Publishers, Inc.**
**P.O. Box 310**
**Shippensburg, PA 17257-0310**

"Speaking to the Purposes of God for This Generation
and for the Generations to Come"

ISBN 0-7684-2021-0
For Worldwide Distribution
Printed in Hong Kong

9 10 11 12 13 14 15 16 17 18 / 10 09 08 07 06 05 04

This book and all other Destiny Image, Revival Press, Mercy Place, Fresh Bread, Destiny Image Fiction, and Treasure House books are available at Christian bookstores and distributors worldwide.

For a U.S. bookstore nearest you, call **1-800-722-6774**.
For more information on foreign distributors, call **717-532-3040**.
Or reach us on the Internet: **http://www.destinyimage.com**

# THE WRITER

Dian Layton has been telling stories to children of all ages for more than 20 years. But when Destiny Image Publishers asked her to write a children's version of *Hinds' Feet on High Places*, it was a new adventure for her: "It has always been a favorite of mine—it was a wonderful idea!" Dian determined to write something that would please Hannah Hurnard, the author, if she were alive today. Careful to remain true to the original story, Dian's adaptation is easier to understand and is more applicable to children. Simple devotionals help parents teach their children the important truths woven throughout the story.

Dian Layton has written several books and musical productions, and has produced numerous cassette recordings. She ministers throughout Canada and the United States. A native of Alberta, Canada, Dian now lives in Shippensburg, Pennsylvania, with her husband, Barry, and their two young sons, Benjamin and Jonathan.

## THE ARTIST

JoAnn Edington painted 70 individual paintings to produce this colorful masterpiece, an adapted *Hinds' Feet on High Places* based on Hannah Hurnard's timeless classic. JoAnn first read *Hinds' Feet on High Places* at the age of 17, and was so captivated by the similarities in the tale with her own life that she purchased several copies and gave them to her family and friends. She has poured years of personal reflection, experience, and artistic skill into this new classic for children.

JoAnn lives in Colorado with her husband, Max, and their two daughters, Kimberly and Hannah. Born and raised in Northern Pennsylvania, JoAnn was introduced to the Shepherd by her mother, Verna, years ago, and has lived in His High Places ever since.

## THE GRAPHIC DESIGNER

Tony Laidig has assembled *Hinds' Feet on High Places* in its entirety. Tony crafted every page so the beautiful illustrations that appear on each page would correspond to the delightful storyline. Tony's desire to push the computer to its limits has enabled this project to be assembled entirely on computer.

Tony resides in Scotland, Pennsylvania, with his wife, Debbie, and their two daughters, Ashlea and Courtney. He returned to this area following the Shepherd's leading.

# Table of Contents

# Chapter 1
## *In the Village of Much-Trembling*

This is the story of a young girl named Much-Afraid who learned to trust the Chief Shepherd. It is the story of how she left her Fearing relatives and went with the Shepherd to the High Places where "perfect love gets rid of fear."

Much-Afraid lived in a peaceful little white cottage in the Valley of Humiliation. She had many friends who lived in the same Village as she

did. Many of her neighbors in the Village of Much-Trembling worked for the Chief Shepherd. For several years Much-Afraid herself had been in His service.

She loved her work and really wanted to make the Shepherd happy, but in her heart, Much-Afraid worried. She worried about her crippled body. Her feet were so crooked that she limped and often fell down as she went about her work. She also worried about her mouth. It too was so crooked that it was hard for her to speak clearly. Much-Afraid felt that she was not very pretty.

More than anything else, Much-Afraid wanted to be beautiful, graceful, and strong, like so many of the Shepherd's other workers. In fact, she wanted to be like the Chief Shepherd Himself, but she was afraid that would never be possible.

There was another, even greater trouble in her life. Much-Afraid was a member of the Family of Fearings, and her relatives lived all over the Valley. She could never get away from them.

Much-Afraid was an orphan and had grown up in the home of her aunt, poor Mrs. Dismal Forebodings. (Dismal Forebodings means always being afraid and worried about all the terrible things that might happen.) So Much-Afraid had lived with her aunt and her cousins Gloomy and Spiteful and their brother

Craven Fear. (Craven means to be *very* afraid.) He was a bully who always did mean things to Much-Afraid.

The Family of Fearings hated the Chief Shepherd and were very upset that Much-Afraid was one of His servants. They kept trying to make her quit working for Him.

Then, one awful day, her relatives came to the cottage where Much-Afraid lived and announced that she was to marry Craven Fear! What a horrible idea! She should have ordered them all to leave her cottage, but poor Much-Afraid listened to her Fearing relatives. She just sat cowering before them, repeating again and again that nothing would ever make her marry Craven Fear.

When they finally left her alone, it was early evening. Suddenly, Much-Afraid thought of something that made her feel happier. The Chief Shepherd would be bringing His flocks of sheep to the watering place beside the Village! Much-Afraid met Him there every morning to learn His wishes for the day, and again in the evenings to give Him her report on the day's work.

Still shaking with fear, she came to the pool where the Shepherd was wait-ing for her. She told Him what her Family of Fearings had said.

"What can I do?" she cried. "They can't really make me

marry Craven, can they? Oh! It is bad enough to be Much-Afraid! I couldn't stand to be Mrs. Craven Fear for the rest of my life!"

"Don't be afraid," the Shepherd said gently. "You are in My service, and if you trust Me, they will not be able to force you." He paused for a moment, then continued, "Much-Afraid, you should never have let your Fearing relatives into your cottage. They are enemies of the King whom you serve."

"I know, oh, I know," cried Much-Afraid, "but whenever I meet any of my relatives, I feel so weak! As long as I live in the Valley, I will keep meeting them. They are everywhere! Now I will be too afraid to leave my cottage."

Much-Afraid looked across the Valley and river to the beautiful mountains. She cried out with all her heart, "Oh, if only I could leave this Valley and go to the High Places! The Fearings and my other relatives could never reach me there!"

To her great surprise the Shepherd answered, "I have waited a long time to hear you say those words, Much-Afraid. It would be best for you to leave the Valley and go to the High Places. You need to live in the Kingdom of Love. No fears of any kind are there because 'perfect love gets rid of fear.'"

Much-Afraid stared at Him in amazement. "Go to the High Places," she exclaimed, "and live there? Oh, if only I could! For months I have been thinking about it, day and night, but it's not possible. I could never get there. I am too crippled." She looked down at her crooked feet and her eyes filled with tears. "The mountains are so steep and dangerous. I have been told that only deer can move on them safely."

6

(Dear Reader: From now on we will refer to deer as "harts" and "hinds." Harts are a kind of male deer and hinds are female.)

"It is quite true that the way up to the High Places is both difficult and dangerous," said the Shepherd. "It has to be, so that nothing which is an enemy of love can get into the Kingdom. Nothing crippled or deformed is allowed, and the people who live there do need 'hinds' feet.' I have them Myself," He added with a smile, "and I can go leaping on the mountains with the greatest of ease and pleasure. Much-Afraid, I could make your feet like hinds' feet too and set you upon the High Places. You could then serve Me much better and be out of reach of all your enemies."

Much-Afraid stared at Him. "Make my feet like hinds' feet," she repeated. "How is that possible? And what about my crooked, ugly mouth?"

"It is true," said the Shepherd, "that you would have to be changed before you could live on the High Places, but if you are willing to go with Me, I promise to help you. Up on the mountains, as you get closer to the High Places, the air is so clean that it will strengthen your whole body. There are healing streams where everything that is not beautiful is washed away.

"There is something else I must tell you. No member of the Fearing family can enter the Kingdom of Love. You will have to be given a new name first. Are you willing, Much-Afraid, to be changed completely, and to be made like the new name you will receive?"

She nodded her head and said, "Yes, I am."

The Shepherd put His hand upon her heart, and she felt sweetness and pain mixed together. "I plant the seed of love in your heart," He said. "When it blooms, you will receive a new name.

"There is one more thing I must tell you. I will take you to the foot of the mountains Myself, so that there will be no danger from your enemies. From then on, you will not see Me all the time, Much-Afraid, but I will be able to hear you whenever you speak to Me. Whenever you call for help I promise to come to you at once. Two special helpers will guide you on the steep and hard places while your feet are still crippled and you can only go slowly. I have chosen them Myself. Will you accept them with joy and let them be your helpers?"

"Oh, yes," she answered at once, smiling at Him happily. "Of course I am quite certain that You know best, and whatever You choose is right." Then she added joyfully, "I feel like I will never be afraid again!"

The Shepherd looked at her very kindly. No one understood better than He that growing into the likeness of a new name takes a long, long time. But He did not tell her so. Instead He said, "Now you may go home and get ready. Do not tell anyone about your journey to the High Places. It needs to be a secret. Be ready to come when I call."

10

# Spend Some Quiet Time

## Think About:

This story is an "allegory." That means it is something like the parables that Jesus told. The characters and places illustrate (make a picture of) something we need to learn. For example:

1. Who is the Shepherd? He's Jesus!

2. Who is Much-Afraid? (Hmm, I wonder....) Much-Afraid is actually someone inside each one of us! Jesus, our Chief Shepherd, wants us to be strong on the inside, in our "spirit-man." Much-Afraid is crippled and not very pretty. God wants us to be healthy and beautiful inside; the outside doesn't matter nearly so much.

3. Who are the Fearing relatives? Inside every person are fears, worries, wrong habits, etc., that we need to be set free from.

4. What are the High Places? No, not Heaven. In the final chapter, you'll find Heaven referred to as the "Highest Places." Jesus wants us to be strong and healthy in our spirit-man, free from our enemies, long before we get to Heaven! He wants us to learn how to be on top of our problems like a deer leaps on the mountains! He wants us to live a "victorious Christian life" here.

5. Why was the journey to the High Places a secret? What happens inside your spirit-man is seen only by you and the Lord. People see the outside, where you might look as if you are doing just great, but He looks at your heart.

## Read the Great Book (the Bible):

1 Samuel 16:7 — God sees my heart.

Psalm 18:33 — He makes my feet like a deer's...

Habakkuk 3:19 — ...so I can go on the High Places.

Psalm 18:3 — I will call upon the Lord...He will save me from my enemies.

## Pray:

"Jesus, sometimes I too am 'Much-Afraid.' Help me to trust You as my Shepherd. Please help my spirit-man not to be crippled and afraid. I want to be strong on the inside for You. As I read these chapters, please help me understand what they mean. Let the words make pictures in my heart of what lessons You want me to learn. Bye for now!"

Much-Afraid left her meeting with the Shepherd, feeling as though she would never be afraid again. She began to sing one of her favorite songs from the Great Book, the Book that the shepherds loved to sing from as they worked among the flocks and led them through the fields. Happily she walked along, when suddenly she saw Craven Fear.

Poor Much-Afraid. Her heart filled with a terrible panic. She looked right and left, but there was no place to hide. Craven Fear was coming right toward her.

"Well, here you are at last, little Much-Afraid. So, we are to be married! What do you think of that?" He pinched her, as though trying to play, but it hurt her very much. Then he grabbed her, and poor Much-Afraid cried out in pain. Suddenly, Craven Fear let go of her and backed away.

The Shepherd was there! One look at His flashing eyes and uplifted shepherd's staff was more than enough for that bully. Craven Fear turned and ran away.

Much-Afraid started to cry. Of course she should have known that Craven Fear was a coward! All she needed to do was call for the Shepherd, and that bully would have run away at once. Now her dress was torn, her arms were bruised, and her heart was full of shame.

She didn't dare look at the Shepherd. She supposed that He too was thinking how silly she was to be so afraid. But, if she had looked, she would have seen how tenderly the Shepherd watched her as she limped toward the Village.

Much-Afraid woke early the next morning and all her fears were gone. Her first thought was about the Shepherd. Probably sometime today she would start for the High Places with Him! This so excited her that she could hardly eat her breakfast, and as she began getting ready for her journey, she sang a song from the Shepherd's Great Book. All morning, whenever she thought of the Shepherd, she would run to the door or the window to see if He was coming to call her.

By noon He still had not come, but some others came. All of a sudden, before she realized what was happening, there was a trampling of feet and many noisy voices, and then she was surrounded by a whole army of aunts, uncles, and cousins. Leading the pack was Aunt Dismal and her daughters, Gloomy and Spiteful. Next was Lord Fearing himself, followed by Coward. They rushed right into her cottage and locked the door.

The whole family talked on and on about how she needed to spend more time with her relatives, and how marriage to Craven would be the best thing for her to do. They told her that she could help him become a kinder and better person. Much-Afraid sat and listened to their voices.

Suddenly, they all heard something outside.

In the distance was the sound of a Man singing one of the songs from the Book which Much-Afraid loved so well. Then the Singer Himself came in view, slowly passing along the lane. It was the Chief Shepherd, already leading His flock to the watering place.

As she listened to His song, Much-Afraid realized that the Shepherd was calling her to go with Him! But here she was, locked in with her terrible Fears and unable to respond to His call! She did not realize that the Fearings were holding their breath in case she would respond—because if she did they would all run wildly out the door! Poor Much-Afraid was too frightened to call, and then it was too late.

The next moment she felt Coward's heavy hand over her mouth and many other hands tightly holding her down on the chair. When they were very sure the Shepherd was gone, they let her go, and realized Much-Afraid had fainted. They would have carried her away right then and there, but decided it was too dangerous. The people of the Village would soon be returning from their work. The Fearings decided to wait until dark, when no one could see them. Then they would take her to marry Craven Fear.

They laid Much-Afraid on her bed and started to look through her cupboards for something to eat. Gloomy was told to watch Much-Afraid in case she woke up.

Gradually she did wake up and nearly fainted again when she saw her cottage still full of Fearing relatives! She didn't dare call for help because all her neighbors were away at work—but were they? Just then she heard the voice of her neighbor, Mrs. Valiant. (Valiant means to be very, very brave!)

Gloomy was quite unprepared for what happened next. Suddenly, Much-Afraid jumped out of her bed and shouted through the window as loudly as she could, "Valiant! Valiant! Come and help me. Come quickly! Help!"

Mrs. Valiant looked across the garden and saw Much-Afraid's terrified face at the window. The next moment the face was jerked away, and the curtain was closed. That was enough for Mrs. Valiant. She hurried to the cottage and tried to open the door. Finding it locked, she looked in through a window and saw the room full of Much-Afraid's relatives.

That brave lady put her head right in through the open window and cried out with a loud voice, "Out of this house you go, this minute, every one of you! If you are not gone in three seconds, I will call the Chief Shepherd. This cottage belongs to Him, and you'll be in big trouble if He finds you here!"

Immediately, the door was unlocked and out poured the Fearings, tumbling over each other in their hurry to get away!

Mrs. Valiant smiled in satisfaction as she watched them run. Then she went into the cottage to Much-Afraid, who was still shaking with fear, and heard the whole story of what had happened.

Mrs. Valiant made her a nice hot cup of tea and fixed her supper from the food the Fearings had been ready to eat. Then she cleaned up the mess the unwelcome visitors had made and tucked Much-Afraid into bed.

Before leaving the cottage, Mrs. Valiant put a bell beside the bed. "If you need help during the night, just ring that bell," she told Much-Afraid, "and the whole Valiant family will come over right away!"

Then Mrs. Valiant left, carefully locking the cottage door and taking the extra key that Much-Afraid had given to her. For hours Much-Afraid lay in her bed, unable to sleep. Her body was bruised, and her mind was troubled. *There was something important I was supposed to do*, she thought. But she couldn't remember what it was. Finally, she fell asleep.

She woke suddenly an hour or two later and sat straight up in her bed. The place in her

18

heart where the Shepherd had planted the seed of love was throbbing with pain. Now she remembered what had bothered her before she had fallen asleep! The Shepherd had called as He promised, but she hadn't gone to Him or even answered! What if He thought she had changed her mind and didn't want to go with Him? What if He had already gone and left her behind?

The shock of that thought was awful. Much-Afraid had to see for herself at once if He had really gone away and left without her. She got out of bed, dressed as quickly as her shaking fingers would let her, and unlocked the cottage door.

Opening the door, she went out into the darkness. A hundred Craven Fears on the lonely streets of Much-Trembling could not have stopped her at that moment, as Much-Afraid started off to look for the Shepherd.

She went as quickly as possible with her crooked feet, limping along the village streets toward the open fields and the sheepfolds, toward the watering place. It was almost dawn. Would He be there?

Just as the sky turned red above the mountains, she saw Him. He was there, standing by the pool, looking toward her with the light of the sunrise shining on His face.

As Much-Afraid stumbled toward Him, He stepped quickly to her side. She fell down at His feet, sobbing, "Oh, my Shepherd, take me with You as You said. Don't leave me behind."

"I knew you would come," He said gently, "but Much-Afraid, why were you not here at the pool as usual last evening? Didn't you hear Me when I passed your cottage and called? I wanted you to be ready to start with Me this morning at sunrise."

"I am here now," said Much-Afraid, still kneeling at His feet, "and I will go with You anywhere."

Then the Shepherd took her by the hand and they started toward the mountains.

# Spend Some Quiet Time

## Think About:

Why were Much-Afraid's relatives able to enter her cottage? Who are your enemies? What do you battle with? Fear, worry, wrong thoughts, selfishness…? Have you ever felt your heart fill with fear? When it happens again, what will you do?

Much-Afraid had a special place where she met with the Shepherd every day. I like to think of this as the "Secret Place" where I can go and talk to Jesus. He is always there. I don't see Him, but He is always there! I can tell Him how I really feel inside. Do you have a special place where you can go every day to spend time with the Lord?

## Memorize:

"Go into the Secret Place and shut the door; your heavenly Father hears your prayer—He will reward! Matthew 6:6." Say it till it sticks! (Say this with a rhythm!)

## Pray:

"Jesus, You know all about me. You know what enemies come into my cottage, in my heart. Please help me keep the door locked, and not to let them in! When I do meet them, help me not to listen to them, but to call for Your help right away! And Lord, please help me to spend time with You every day in my 'Secret Place.' Bye for now!"

# Chapter 2

## *Beginning the Journey*

It was the early morning of a beautiful day. Most of the Valley was asleep. The only sounds were the joyful laughter of the running streams and the happy little songs of birds. The dew sparkled on the grass, and the flowers glowed like little jewels. Sometimes the Shepherd and Much-Afraid walked over patches of thousands of blossoms that looked like a carpet in a king's palace.

Much-Afraid looked at the Shepherd. "Sometimes I have wondered about the wild flowers," she said. "It seems strange that they should grow in places like this where the goats and cattle walk all over them. They have so much beauty and sweetness to give, and hardly anyone sees them."

The look the Shepherd turned on her was very beautiful. "Nothing that My Father and I have made is ever wasted," He said quietly, "and the wild flowers have a wonderful lesson to teach. Many people live a quiet, ordinary life. Hardly anyone even knows about them, but their hearts are like delightful gardens where the King Himself walks and rejoices. Some of My servants have won great respect from other people and are famous, but always their greatest victories are like the wild flowers, those which

no one knows about. Learn this lesson now, down here in the Valley, Much-Afraid, and when you get to the steep places of the mountains it will comfort you."

Then He added, "Come, the birds are all singing so happily. Let's sing too!" So as they walked, they sang together one of the old songs from the Shepherd's Great Book. Just as they finished singing, they came to a place where a rushing stream poured itself across the path they were following and went tumbling down the other side. It was running so swiftly and singing so loudly that it seemed to fill the Valley around them with its laughing voice.

As the Shepherd lifted Much-Afraid across the slippery, wet stones she said to Him, "I do wish I knew what it is that all running water sings. Sometimes I lie in bed at night and listen to the little stream that runs past the cottage garden. It sounds so happy and seems to sing over and over again some lovely secret message. Tell me, Shepherd, do You know what the waters sing as they hurry on their way?"

The Shepherd smiled, and they stood there quietly for a few minutes. Suddenly, as Much-Afraid stood beside the Shepherd, it seemed as

though, bit by bit, the water
language became clear. It is, of course,
impossible to write it in water language, but this is the best I can do to
translate it:

### The Water Song

*Come, oh come! Let us away—*
*Lower and lower every day.*
*From the heights we leap and flow*
*To the valleys down below.*
*Always answering to the call,*
*To the lowest place of all.*

"I don't understand," said Much-Afraid after she had listened for a
while. "The water seems to be singing so gladly because it is hurrying to
go down into the Valley, and yet You are calling me to the High Places.
What does it mean?"

"The High Places," answered the Shepherd, "are the starting place. It is
only up on the High Places of Love that anyone can receive the power to
pour himself out and give to others."

Much-Afraid still didn't really understand, but now as she listened, she
heard the wild flowers singing the same sort of song.

*This is the law by which we live—*
*It is so sweet to give and give.*

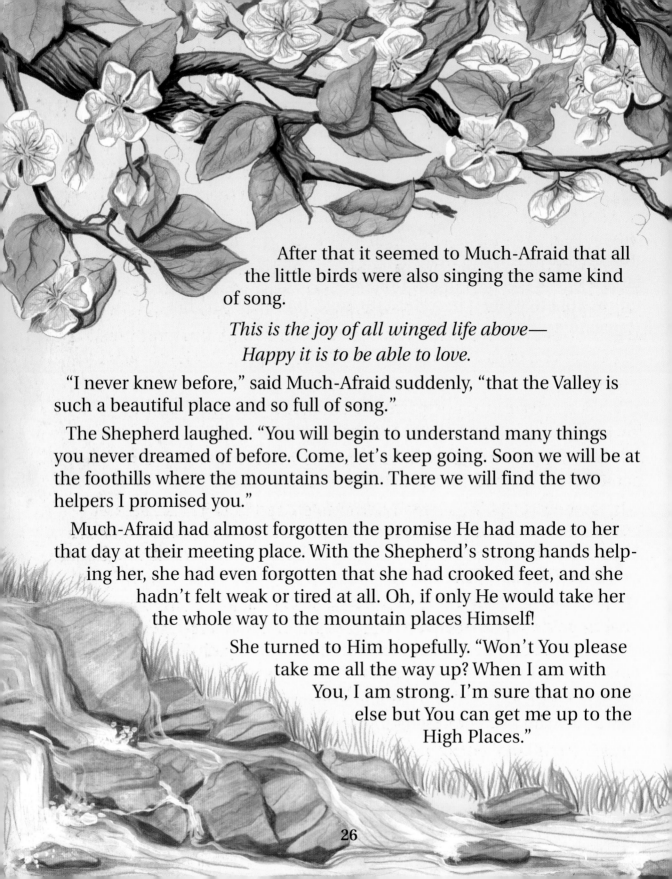

After that it seemed to Much-Afraid that all the little birds were also singing the same kind of song.

*This is the joy of all winged life above—*
*Happy it is to be able to love.*

"I never knew before," said Much-Afraid suddenly, "that the Valley is such a beautiful place and so full of song."

The Shepherd laughed. "You will begin to understand many things you never dreamed of before. Come, let's keep going. Soon we will be at the foothills where the mountains begin. There we will find the two helpers I promised you."

Much-Afraid had almost forgotten the promise He had made to her that day at their meeting place. With the Shepherd's strong hands helping her, she had even forgotten that she had crooked feet, and she hadn't felt weak or tired at all. Oh, if only He would take her the whole way to the mountain places Himself!

She turned to Him hopefully. "Won't You please take me all the way up? When I am with You, I am strong. I'm sure that no one else but You can get me up to the High Places."

26

He looked at her most kindly, but answered quietly, "Much-Afraid, I could do what you wish. I could carry you all the way, instead of having you climb there. But if I did, you would never develop hinds' feet, become My companion, and go where I go. If you climb with the helpers I have chosen for you, even though it will seem like a very long and hard journey, I promise that you will develop hinds' feet. Then you will be able to run and jump with Me, far away from your enemies.

"Some of them, you know, can visit the lower parts of the mountains. You will probably meet them as you begin to climb. That is why I have most carefully chosen for you two of the very best and strongest helpers. And, as I promised you before, even though you won't see Me, I will always be there. Whenever you call for help, I promise to come to you at once."

"You will give me a new name when I get to the top?" asked Much-Afraid with a quivering voice.

"When the flower of love blooms in your heart, you will receive a new name," He answered softly. "Remember My promise?"

She remembered. Was it really just yesterday when He had planted love in her heart and promised that she would be changed from Much-Afraid? She looked into the eyes of the Shepherd. "I will trust You and do whatever You want," she said.

In a very short time they crossed a bridge at the foot of the mountains. Here huge rocks were scattered all around, and suddenly Much-Afraid saw two women sitting on one of the rocks by the path. They both wore veils over their faces. As the Shepherd and Much-Afraid came closer, the two stood up and bowed silently to Him.

"Here are the two helpers I promised you," said the Shepherd quietly.

Much-Afraid looked at them fearfully. They were tall and looked very strong, but why did they wear veils? Why were they hiding their faces?

Why didn't they say anything?

"Who are they?" she whispered to the Shepherd. "Will You tell me their names? Why don't they say anything? Can't they speak?"

"Yes, they can speak," said the Shepherd very quietly, "but they speak a new language, Much-Afraid. It is a language of the mountains which you have not learned yet. But as you travel with them, little by little, you will learn to understand their words.

"They are two of the best teachers I have. This," He said, motioning to the first of the silent women, "is Sorrow. The other is her twin sister, Suffering."

Poor Much-Afraid! She grew very pale and began to tremble. She felt as if she would faint and hung on tightly to the Shepherd.

"I can't go with them!" she cried. "I can't! I can't! Oh Shepherd, why must You make Sorrow and Suffering be my helpers? Can't Joy and Peace go with me? They would make me strong and help me be happy on my journey! I never thought You would do this to me!" She burst into tears.

He answered her very gently. "Will you

trust Me, Much-Afraid? Will you go with them, or do you want to go back to the Valley, to all your Fearing relatives—to Craven Fear himself?"

Much-Afraid shook at the thought. What a terrible choice to have to make. She knew Fear very well, but Suffering and Sorrow seemed terrifying. How could she go with them? Then she looked at the Shepherd and suddenly realized how very much she loved Him. Even if He asked the impossible, she would do it.

"Do I want to go back?" she asked. "Oh, Shepherd, who would I go to? In all the world I have no one but You. Help me to do what You ask. Help me to trust You!"

As He heard these words the Shepherd suddenly lifted His head and laughed—a laugh full of delight and victory. It echoed round the rocky walls and for a moment it seemed that the mountains were laughing with Him.

Then He spoke. "Fear not, Much-Afraid, only believe. Go with Sorrow and Suffering. When you come to hard places, put your hands in theirs and they will lead you exactly where I want you to go."

She stepped forward, looking at the two veiled women, and said with a courage she had never felt before, "I will go with you.

Please lead the way." But she could not bring herself to take their hands in hers.

The Shepherd laughed again. "Remember My promise to bring you to the High Places and to make your feet like hinds' feet!"

He handed them a sack filled with food and water for their journey. Then He jumped on to a great rock at the side of the path and from there to another and to yet another. The Shepherd went leaping up the mountains until He was out of sight.

Much-Afraid started out, limping toward the High Places, pretending not to see the outstretched hands of her helpers, Sorrow and Suffering.

# Spend Some Quiet Time

## Think About:

You and I probably feel like Much-Afraid does about Sorrow and Suffering. We would much rather have Joy and Peace in our lives than any kind of trouble or pain. Do you know people who love the Lord, but who still went through lots of sadness and pain? Maybe they were very sick, or someone close to them died. What kind of person are they?

We have a choice to make when Sorrow and Suffering come our way. We can get upset and angry...or we can thank God and trust Him to take care of us. We can let the troubles in our lives be used to make our spirit-man stronger.

## Read the Great Book:

Isaiah 53:3-5 — Jesus knew Sorrow and Suffering.

Psalm 119:71 — Trouble can be good for us!

Psalm 46:1 — God is with us in times of trouble.

## Pray:

"Thank You, Lord, for how You suffered for me. When things happen that hurt me or make me feel sad, please help me to trust You. Use the Sorrow and Suffering that I meet to make my spirit-man stronger. Amen."

From the very beginning the mountains were steeper than Much-Afraid could handle on her own. It wasn't very long until she reached out to her helpers. Each time she took hold of the hand of either Sorrow or Suffering, a sharp pain went through her. But once she held on tightly, their hands felt very strong. They seemed to be able to pull and even lift her up and over places that she thought looked impossible.

It was not very long, too, before she realized that she needed their help in another way. To her surprise and distress there were enemies along the way.

You see, back down in the Valley that had been Much-Afraid's home, all her Fearing relatives were very upset. To think that she had escaped from the Valley and actually gone off to the mountains with the Shepherd they hated so much! Ugly, crippled little Much-Afraid! Why should she get to go and live on the High Places?

Maybe she would even be given a place of service in the palace of the great King Himself! It was not that they wanted to go to the mountains themselves, but it was terrible to think of Much-Afraid going!

They had a big meeting to decide how they would capture her and bring her back to the Valley to be their slave. But how could they do that? She was under the protection of the Great Shepherd. Somehow, they would have to trick her into wanting to return for herself.

Finally it was decided. They would send a distant cousin to try. He was strong and powerful and very handsome. His name was Pride. He would be the best one to coax Much-Afraid away from the Shepherd. And he would not give up easily. He would be too proud to return to the Valley without her. So the matter was settled.

Much-Afraid and her helpers had been on their journey for only a few days. One morning they turned a corner on the rocky path and there was Pride walking toward them with a big smile. Much-Afraid was very surprised to see him and even more surprised when he greeted her. In the past he had always ignored her, with his nose tilted in the air.

"Well, Cousin Much-Afraid, here you are at last! I've been trying to catch up with you."

Of course, she should have known better than to stop and speak to one of her relatives from the Valley. But it made Much-Afraid feel good to have the handsome

young man actually wanting to talk to her, after being ignored for years. "How do you do, Cousin Pride?" she asked.

"Much-Afraid," said Pride, taking her hand in his, "I have come to try to help you." (The path was at that point not quite so steep and Much-Afraid had let go of Sorrow's and Suffering's hands.) "My dear cousin, you must quit this journey and come back to the Valley with me. Do you know what will happen to you if you keep going? All those promises the Shepherd has made about taking you to His Kingdom and making you live happily ever after won't come true! When He gets you up to the far parts of the mountains, He will leave you there! For the rest of your life, people will make fun of you!"

Poor Much-Afraid now tried to pull her hand free, but Pride held on even more tightly. She had chosen to listen to him, now it would be very hard to get away.

Besides, hadn't she been secretly thinking those same thoughts? What if the Shepherd didn't keep His promises? What if people did make fun of her for believing Him? She hated what Pride was saying, but with him holding her hand so powerfully it was easy to believe his words.

"Come back, Much-Afraid," he urged. "Give it up before it is too late. What is up there that could be worth this difficult journey?"

"I am looking for the Kingdom of Love. The

Shepherd will make my feet like hinds' feet and I will run and leap on the High Places," she whispered.

"You?" he sneered. "Don't you know how ugly and deformed you are? Why, even in the Valley no one loves you! How can you expect to live in the Kingdom of Love? They say nothing but beauty can live there. Come on. Be honest with yourself. Turn back with me before it is too late."

Poor Much-Afraid! The desire to turn back was almost overpowering at that moment. Pride held her tightly, and his words sounded so true. But then, in her heart, she saw the Shepherd. She remembered the look in His eyes when He said, "Remember My promise to bring you to the High Places and to make your feet like hinds' feet!" and "I promise that you will receive a new name."

Before Pride could realize what was happening, Much-Afraid cried out, "Come to me, Shepherd! Come quickly!"

There was the sound of loose rattling stones and a great leap, and the next moment the Shepherd was on the path beside them. His eyes were flashing and His shepherd's staff was raised high above His head. He brought the staff down on Pride, who immediately dropped Much-Afraid's hand. Off he ran down the path and around the corner, slipping and stumbling on the stones as he went.

The Shepherd's voice was gentle but firm. "Much-Afraid, why did you let Pride take your hand? If you had been holding the hands of your two helpers, this would never have happened."

She looked at the Shepherd for a long moment. Then for the first time, of her own free will, Much-Afraid held out both her hands to her two helpers. Sorrow and Suffering seemed even more painful friends now, but she held on to them tightly and turned to continue her journey to the High Places.

# Spend Some Quiet Time

## Think About:

Who is Pride? From the beginning of time, Pride has been a great enemy. When you look at stories in the Bible, Pride made many of the Lord's people stumble and fall on their journey (like Adam and Eve, Samson, Saul, Solomon...). Pride is the thing in us that wants to do what we want—not what God wants. Pride says, "I don't need God or anyone else." Pride says, "Me, me, me, me." Pride worries about what other people think more than what God thinks.

The opposite of Pride is Humility. Humility says, "I need God's help."

## Memorize:

"Proverbs 16:18—'Pride goes before a fall'; but when I walk with Jesus I stand both straight and tall."

## Pray:

"Oh, Lord! Help me not to listen to Pride. Help me not to worry about what other people think of me. I want my life to please You. I want to depend on You for everything. I know I can't make it through this life unless You go with me, but with You by my side, I can do all things! (Like make friends, pass tests, obey my parents, clean my room....)"

# Chapter 3

## *Through the Desert and Loneliness*

After meeting Pride, Much-Afraid's poor crooked feet hurt her even more, and the journey to the High Places was slow and painful. As time went on, she still held on tightly to her two helpers, Sorrow and Suffering, and gradually they began to make better progress.

Then one day the path turned a corner, and to Much-Afraid's great surprise, she saw a desert in front of them. As far as the eye could see there was only bare sandy land, except for pyramids rising above the sand dunes. (Pyramids are buildings that look like enormous triangles and are made from stone bricks.)

Sorrow and Suffering started to take her on a steep path leading down toward the desert, but Much-Afraid stopped firmly. "We mustn't go down there. The Shepherd has called me to the High Places!" Still they showed her she was to follow them down the steep pathway.

Much-Afraid looked to the left and right, but there was no other path. All around them were rocky cliffs as straight as walls.

"I can't go down there!" she cried with fear. "He called me up to the High Places, not to an empty desert!" She lifted her voice and called loudly, "Shepherd, come to me! I need You. Come and help me!"

In a moment He was there, standing beside her.

"Shepherd, I can't understand this. The helpers You gave me are trying to lead me toward that desert, turning right away from the High Places! Make a way for us, Shepherd, as You promised."

He answered her very gently. "That is the path, Much-Afraid, and you are to go down there."

"Oh no," she cried. "You can't mean it! You promised to take me to the High Places!"

"Much-Afraid, do You love Me enough to trust Me? Will you go down there with Me, even though the path seems to lead you away from what I have promised?"

She sank to her knees at His feet, sobbing as if her heart would break. "I do love You. You know I do. Oh, forgive me because I can't help crying. I will go with You into the wilderness. I will trust You to choose for me what is best."

So there Much-Afraid built her first altar, a little pile of broken rocks. With the Shepherd standing close beside her, she laid down on the altar her own desires. A little spurt of flame came from somewhere, and then there was nothing but a heap of ashes. That is, at first she thought there was nothing. The Shepherd told her to look closer, and there among the ashes was a little stone.

"Pick it up and take it with you," said the Shepherd, "to remember this altar that you built and all that it stands for." He handed her a little bag. Much-Afraid picked up the stone from the ashes, dropped it into the little bag, and put it away carefully.

Much to her delighted surprise, the Shepherd walked with them down into the desert. He began to sing a song from

the Great Book, and Much-Afraid felt her pain begin to melt away.

They reached the desert quickly because Much-Afraid leaned on the Shepherd. By evening they were at one of the great pyramids. At its base were some little huts where they would spend the night. At sunset, when the sky burned fiery red over the western side of the desert, the Shepherd led Much-Afraid away from the huts to the foot of the pyramid.

"Much-Afraid," He said, "all of My servants had to pass through the desert on their way to the High Places. Here they have learned many things which they could never have learned any other place."

Suddenly the desert was full of people, like an endless parade. Some of them Much-Afraid knew from reading their stories in the Great Book. There was Abraham and Sarah, his wife. They had been strangers in a strange land. Then there was Joseph, whose brothers had turned against him. One after another the crowd of people stretched across the desert. The last one in line held out his hand to her, and Much-Afraid joined those faithful servants who had walked through the wilderness.

After this the Shepherd took her back to the huts to rest for the night.

In the morning, the Shepherd called Much-Afraid again. He led her to a little door in the wall of the pyramid and took her inside. There was a hallway that led to the center, and from there a spiral staircase went to the floors above.

But the Shepherd opened another door on the ground floor, and they went into a large room. Piles of grain were everywhere, except in the middle. There in the open space men were threshing the grain. Much-Afraid watched how the grains were first beaten until they crumbled to pieces. Then they were beaten with stones until they became the finest flour.

(Did you know that is how flour is made? Grain is taken from farmers' fields, the tiny kernels are separated from the husk of leaves that surrounds them, and then they are ground into powdery flour. The flour is used to make bread to eat!)

"It is the same with My people," the Shepherd said gently. "They too must be threshed and ground into the finest powder so they can become like bread for others. It is a painful process."

After this the Shepherd took her back to the central room, and they climbed the spiral staircase. There on the second floor was another, smaller room. In the center was a man making pottery. He was working with soft clay upon a potter's wheel, making a beautiful bowl.

As they watched, the Shepherd said, "I work with My people as though they are clay. I mold and shape them to be like beautiful vessels. I want to do that with you, Much-Afraid. I want you to be as clay in My hands."

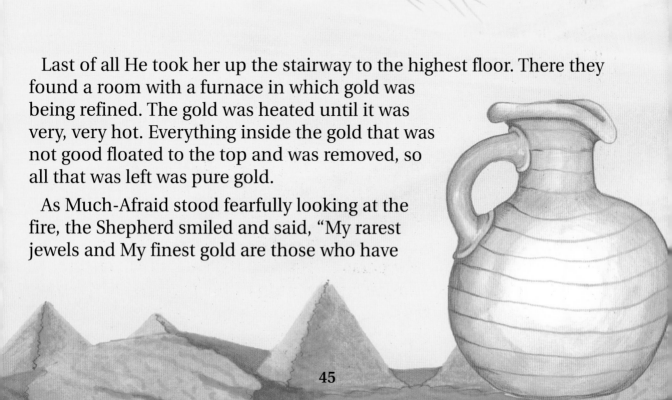

Last of all He took her up the stairway to the highest floor. There they found a room with a furnace in which gold was being refined. The gold was heated until it was very, very hot. Everything inside the gold that was not good floated to the top and was removed, so all that was left was pure gold.

As Much-Afraid stood fearfully looking at the fire, the Shepherd smiled and said, "My rarest jewels and My finest gold are those who have gone through the fire." Then He took her hand in His and continued, "So don't be surprised when you are tested by a fiery trial. Rejoice and be happy!"

"Rejoice and be happy." The words echoed in her mind as Much-Afraid walked back down the staircase, still holding the Shepherd's hand. Then she remembered some other words she had read once in the Great Book. "He knows the way I take. When He has tried me, I shall come forth as pure gold." The words were comforting, and she spoke them over and over in her heart.

They stayed in the desert huts for several days. Time was spent resting and restocking their supply of food and water. On the last morning, Much-Afraid made a lovely discovery as she went for a walk. Behind one of the huts was an old pipe connected to a water tank. In the pipe was a tiny hole from which drops of water fell one by one. At the place where they landed was the first growing thing she had seen in the desert. It was a beautiful little golden flower.

Much-Afraid knelt close to it and asked softly, "What is your name, lovely flower?"

The tiny plant seemed to answer at once with a voice as golden as itself. "I am Acceptance-With-Joy."

Much-Afraid thought of the things she had seen in the pyramid: the threshing-floor, the potter's wheel, and the fiery furnace. The words of the little golden flower echoed in her mind and she said to herself, "I too want to be Acceptance-With-Joy. Whatever He lets me go through, I want to trust Him and allow Him to have His way with my life. And I want to do it with joy in my heart."

Then she stooped down and picked up a pebble that was lying in the sand beside the flower and put it into her little bag with the first altar stone.

## Spend Some Quiet Time

### Think About:

Grain being ground into flour...clay on the potter's wheel...the furnace purifying gold...hmm. None of these sound like much fun, do they?

What does "Acceptance-With-Joy" mean? Every time we feel pressure, and the heat is being turned up on our lives, God wants us to accept *happily* the trials we go through.

The opposite is Murmuring and Complaining. Do you ever do that? When something goes wrong do you say, "Oh, man, why did this have to happen?!" Or do you say, "I don't understand why this happened, but I trust You, Jesus"?

It is much easier to murmur and complain. So we certainly need God's help to become "Acceptance-With-Joy"!

### Read the Great Book:

Isaiah 28:28 — Being like bread

Jeremiah 18:3-4 — The potter's wheel

1 Peter 4:12-13; James 1:2 — *Rejoice* in the fiery trial.

Job 23:10 — When He has tried me I shall come forth as pure gold!

## Pray:

"Oh, Jesus, when bad or hard things happen to me, help me not to get upset and complain. Help me to be Acceptance-With-Joy, and to trust that You are looking after me. You are making me into the person You want me to be. I don't want to be like a lump of hard, dry play dough! I want to be soft clay in Your hands. And I don't want to just be a rock. I want to be a precious stone, pure gold for You. Help me to rejoice when I go through 'fiery trials'! Amen."

uch-Afraid and the Shepherd, together with Suffering and Sorrow, kept walking through the desert. Then one day, quite suddenly, they came to a path. "This," said the Shepherd quietly, "is the way you are to go." So they turned and after a while found themselves on the shore of a great sea.

"It is time for Me to leave you, Much-Afraid," He said, "and return to the mountains. Even though you seem farther away than ever from the High Places, I will still come to you quickly if you call Me." He then went leaping and bounding across the desert toward the mountains which were far behind them.

Much-Afraid and her two helpers walked along the shores of the great sea for many days. She began to know the name of the place where she presently journeyed. It was Loneliness. Now the mountains were out of sight, and her home in the Valley was far, far away. There seemed to be nothing in the whole world except for the desert on one side and the endless, dreary sea on the other. Often an icy wind would blow, and the only sound was the lonely crying of sea gulls overhead.

In those days Much-Afraid never let go of the hands of her two helpers. It was amazing how swiftly they helped her along. It was also amazing how she walked now with hardly a limp. Somehow, something had happened to her in the desert. She was learning to accept with joy the path the Shepherd had for her.

Although she went with Sorrow and Suffering day after day beside the Sea of Loneliness, Much-Afraid felt a happiness in her heart. She even began to realize that the place was strangely beautiful. She spoke words to herself that she had read in the Great Book: "When He has tried me, I shall come forth as gold. Weeping may last for a night, but joy comes in the morning."

Meanwhile, far away in the Valley, her Fearing relatives had been waiting for Pride to come back with Much-Afraid. As time passed they realized he

must not have been able to make her turn around and was now too proud to come back and admit that he had failed. They decided they had to send others to help him, before Much-Afraid reached the High Places and was forever out of their reach.

Spies were sent out to find Pride, and they brought back word that Much-Afraid was nowhere near the mountains, but far away on the shores of Loneliness. This made her relatives very excited. They quickly agreed on who should go and help Pride bring Much-Afraid back to them. Resentment, Bitterness, and Self-Pity left right away.

(Have you ever met those three? Resentment is like Anger. He is even as strong as Hatred. If he ever tries to speak to you, don't listen! His cousin, Bitterness, is a sarcastic, sour fellow. In fact, if you listen to him too much, his words act like poison to your spirit-man. He holds grudges and never forgives. Self-Pity is someone who seems to be around everyone at some time. He tries to get you to feel sorry for your-self. If you ever think things like "poor me" or "no one likes me" or "why

does it always happen to me" watch out! That is Self-Pity talking to you. You need to start thinking about the Lord and other people and quit worrying about yourself!)

Those were the three characters who joined Pride. Off they went to the shores of Loneliness. However, her enemies soon discovered that this was not the same Much-Afraid they used to know. They could not get close to her because she kept so near to Sorrow and Suffering. All they could do was call out to her.

"I told you so!" Pride shouted. "Where are you now, you little fool? Up on the High Places? Ha! He's gone and left you, just like I said He would!"

Resentment raised his ugly head over a rock. "Who is this Shepherd that you follow? Why do you let Him treat you like this? He promised to take you to the High Places, and here you are next to the desert!"

Then Bitterness sneered out from behind another rock, "The more you let Him, the more He will keep doing cruel things to you. You had better turn around and leave Him now, before He asks even more of you."

53

Self-Pity was almost worse than the others. He spoke so softly and in such a whimpering voice that Much-Afraid felt weak all over. "Poor little Much-Afraid," he whispered. "You have every right to feel sorry for yourself. You have been so willing and so obedient, but He keeps thinking up some new way to hurt you and cause such pain."

This last remark was a mistake. The word *pain* suddenly reminded Much-Afraid of the lessons she had learned in the pyramid. The threshing-floor, the potter's wheel, the fiery furnace—all would cause pain, but it was necessary if she wanted to be changed into what the Shepherd wanted her to be. When she thought of this, to Self-Pity's shock, she picked up a piece of rock and threw it at him with all her might!

But she became more and more tired of listening to the voices of her enemies. She couldn't hold her ears because Sorrow and Suffering were holding her hands. It was getting harder to resist their whining, and she was getting weaker. Finally, Much-Afraid had enough.

"Shepherd!" she called. "Come and help me! Hurry!"

To the horror of her enemies, there was the Shepherd, leaping toward them.

Immediately they ran in different directions, trying to escape.

"Oh, Shepherd, thank You! I didn't call You sooner because I thought I could get rid of them myself. Why couldn't I do it?"

"I think," said the Shepherd gently, "that lately you were beginning to tell yourself that it was time I led you back toward the mountains and the High Places. Perhaps you have been Impatient instead of Acceptance-With-Joy. Perhaps...you liked what they said."

Much-Afraid felt her cheeks getting hot. The Shepherd was right. She put her hand into His. "I have been thinking that You have led me on this path too long and that You had forgotten Your promises. I'm sorry. You are my Shepherd. I will trust You and follow where You lead me."

The Shepherd stooped down and picked up a stone which was lying beside her feet. He smiled and said, "Put this in your bag with the other stones. It will help you remember your promise to wait patiently until I do what I have said I would do."

Much-Afraid and her helpers walked for many, many days along the shores of Loneliness. Pride, Resentment, Bitterness, and Self-Pity kept attacking her, but Much-Afraid was getting stronger. She kept remembering to accept the path with joy, no matter what, and to trust the Shepherd.

Finally they arrived at a different place. It was a lovely country filled with fruit trees and hills. Everywhere she looked there were singing birds and blossoming flowers. She felt as though she had stepped out of winter and into spring!

In a short while they came to the edge of some trees, and Much-Afraid gave a little cry of joy. There was the Shepherd, waiting to meet them! She ran toward Him as though she had wings on her feet.

"Oh, welcome, welcome, a thousand times welcome!" she cried, throwing herself into His big strong arms.

"I have come to bring you a message," said the Shepherd, as He held her. "It is time for you to see what I will do."

"Oh, Shepherd," she cried as she pulled away from Him a bit and looked into His eyes, "do You mean that I am finally going to the High Places?"

She thought He nodded, but He didn't answer her. He just stood looking at her with a soft sort of smile.

"Do You mean it?" she asked. "Do You mean that soon

You will be taking me to the High Places?"

This time He answered. "Yes," and added with a strange smile, "now you will see what I will do." He held her for another moment before leaving them, and Much-Afraid felt as though strength was pouring into her.

Much-Afraid had a song in her heart as she walked among the fields and trees of that country. She continued on her happy journey for some time. One day they reached the top of one of the hills just as the sun was rising. There, not far away, were the mountains! Much-Afraid thought she had never seen anything so beautiful.

Finally after such a long time, the path that Much-Afraid and her two helpers traveled had turned toward the High Places! Much-Afraid fell on her knees and worshiped. It seemed to her at that moment that all the pain and all the troubles had been worthwhile.

It seemed to her, also, that even Sorrow and Suffering were smiling with her. Then Much-Afraid realized something else. She was beginning to understand the language spoken by these two sisters. She remembered what the Shepherd had told her when she first met Sorrow and Suffering: "...as you travel with them, little by little, you will learn to understand their words."

As she rose to her feet, Much-Afraid took their hands in hers, and the three travelers started their journey once again.

# Spend Some Quiet Time

## Think About:

When is it hard for you to trust God?

What makes you feel impatient?

Do you ever feel angry at God?

These feelings happen to everyone. Pride, Resentment, Bitterness, and Self-Pity talk to each one of us. It is very important that we don't listen to them. It is much better if we listen to God's Word. Sometimes we do wonder if things will ever work out and if following God's way is the best. Here is what to do:

## Memorize:

"Don't listen to those enemy lies; just say Proverbs 3 verse 5! 'Trust in the Lord with all your heart, don't lean on your own thoughts and mind.'" (Say this with rhythm and actions!)

## Pray:

"Lord, You know what goes on inside my head. You know how hard it is to trust You when it looks like You aren't with me, or when it seems as if You aren't going to answer my prayers. Help me not to just look at what I see with my eyes. Teach me to walk by faith trusting You. Your ways are higher than mine. You will do what is right and good for me, though not always the way I think You should. Help me not to listen to Pride, Resentment, Bitterness, or Self-Pity. Help me to fill my head and heart with Your words and listen to what You say! Bye for now!"

# Chapter 4

## *Up the Mountain of Injury*

Finally, Much-Afraid was traveling toward the High Places. It was amazing how quickly she went with her strong helpers, Sorrow and Suffering. The path was quite smooth, and before long they were near the mountains. As they got closer, Much-Afraid began to worry. The mountains looked so steep!

In the late afternoon the path led them to the rocky cliffs. In every direction the

61

mountains were like walls that went straight up. The cliffs completely blocked their path. There was no sign of a track anywhere, and it would be impossible for them to climb. They would have to turn back.

Just then, Suffering pointed to the rocky walls. Two deer were leaping up the cliff. The hart led the way, and the hind followed him exactly. They leaped and sprang in perfect ease up and up the rocky wall and disappeared over the top. Much-Afraid began to tremble, and her knees shook.

Suffering and Sorrow took her hands in theirs. "Do not be afraid. We don't have to turn around after all! The hart and the hind have shown us the way. We will just follow where they went!"

"Oh, no! No!" Much-Afraid cried out. "It is impossible! The deer may be able to go up there, but I certainly can't! I would be sure to fall on all those awful rocks!" She began sobbing. "I can't do it; I can't! I'll never be able to get to the High Places!" And she crouched to the ground, completely exhausted.

They heard a crunching sound and a rattling of loose stones, then a voice close beside her.

"Ha, ha! My dear little cousin, we meet again at last!"

Much-Afraid found herself looking right in the face of Craven Fear!

"You little fool!" he continued. "Did you really think that you could escape me for good? No, no, Much-Afraid, you are one of the Fearings. You will always be one of the Fearings! You'll never change! I have come to take you back to the Valley where you belong!"

"I won't go with you," cried Much-Afraid.

"Well, you can take your choice," sneered Craven Fear, pointing up the rocky cliff. "Take a look way, way up there. My, it makes me dizzy just to think of poor little you trying to climb

62

that terrible wall of rock! Just picture yourself slipping and struggling and, oh, what a long way it would be if you happened to fall."

"Much-Afraid," said her helpers, shaking her shoulders gently. "Much-Afraid, you know what to do. Call for help!"

She clung to them and sobbed. "I am afraid to call. I am so afraid that if I call Him, He will tell me that I must go that way, that awful, terrible way! It's impossible! I can't face it. Oh, what should I do?"

Sorrow bent over her and said gently, but firmly, "You must call for Him, Much-Afraid. Call for Him at once."

"I can't," she trembled. "This time I just can't."

Craven Fear stepped forward and laughed loudly. Quickly her two helpers put themselves between him and Much-Afraid. Then Suffering looked at Sorrow who nodded back. Suffering reached and poked Much-Afraid sharply, as only Suffering can. Much-Afraid cried out and looked around helplessly. Then she did what she should have done the moment they had reached the impossible-looking wall. She called to the Shepherd.

"Shepherd! Help me! My fears are more than I can handle." As she lifted her voice, Craven Fear scurried away.

"Hello, Much-Afraid," the Shepherd greeted her brightly. "What is the matter? Don't be afraid. I'm here."

He sounded so cheerful and so full of strength that Much-Afraid felt as if a stream of courage was flowing into her from His presence. She had been worried that He might be angry with her for listening again to her fears. She sat up and looked at Him and saw that He was smiling, with no trace of anger in His face. Thankfulness filled her heart, and the icy fear melted away.

"Much-Afraid," He said gently, "tell Me what is the matter. Why were you so afraid?"

"It is the way You have chosen for me to go," she whispered. "It looks so impossible. I feel like I might faint whenever I look up. The deer can go up there, but not a limping, crippled jellyfish like me."

"But Much-Afraid, what promises did I make to you in the Valley?" the Shepherd asked with a smile.

Much-Afraid looked surprised, then fear crept into her heart again. "You promised You would make my feet like hinds' feet and that I would run and leap on the High Places," she said weakly.

"Well," He answered cheerfully, "the only way to do that is to go on the paths that the hinds use—like this one."

Much-Afraid trembled. "Then, I don't think I want hinds' feet," she said.

Instead of being disappointed, the Shepherd actually laughed! "Oh, yes, you do," He said cheerfully. "I know you better than you know yourself, Much-Afraid! You want hinds' feet very much. In fact, that is why I brought you to this side of the mountains. Here the cliffs are very steep, and the only way up is the tracks that the deer use, so the promise I made to you will start to come true. What did I say to you the last time we met?"

"You said, 'Now you will see what I will do,'" she answered. "But I never dreamed You would do something like this! It's too...it's too..." she fumbled for words, then suddenly burst out laughing. "Why, it just doesn't make sense! Whatever will You do next?"

The Shepherd laughed too. "I love doing things that don't seem

to make sense," He replied. "Why, I don't know anything more delightful than turning weakness into strength, fear into faith, and something crooked into something beautiful! The thing I would most enjoy right now is turning a jellyfish into a mountain goat. That is My special work," He added with great joy in His face. "Taking things—taking Much-Afraid, for example, and changing her into—" He broke off, laughing. "Well, we shall see what she finds herself changed into!"

What a difference the Shepherd had made! A short time ago Much-Afraid had been full of fear and worry. Now she and the Shepherd were sitting together on the rocks laughing!

"Come now, little jellyfish," said the Shepherd, "do you believe that I can change you into a mountain goat and get you to the top of this rocky cliff?"

"Yes," she answered. Then she knelt and built a little altar like the one she had made before going into the desert. On it she laid her will—her desire to do what she wanted instead of what He wanted. Fire came from somewhere, and she found among the ashes a larger and rougher stone than any of the others. She placed it carefully into the little bag and stood up.

The Shepherd spoke. "This cliff leads up to Mount Injury." (Injury means being hurt and treated wrongly.) "On the way here you have been learning the lesson of Acceptance-With-Joy. Now it is time to learn a new lesson. As you meet Injury and overcome it, you will discover what the new lesson is."

The Shepherd gently put His hands on her and blessed her. Then He called her helpers and pulled out a strong rope from a crack in the rocky wall. He carefully tied them together.

66

Sorrow was in front and Suffering behind, with Much-Afraid in the middle, so the two who were so strong and sure-footed went before and after to keep her safe.

Then the Shepherd gave her a small bottle. He told her that if she felt weak or faint on the way up to drink a little from it. The label on the bottle read: "Spirit of Grace and Comfort." Much-Afraid tried a drop or two and immediately felt stronger and ready to begin the climb.

By this time it was late afternoon. The Shepherd told them to begin at once. "There is a cave farther up the cliff, which you can't see from here. You can rest there tonight. If you stay down here tonight, your enemies will be sure to pay you a visit. They won't follow you up the cliff, but," He added warningly, "you will probably meet them again when you have reached the top."

With that He smiled brightly, and Sorrow put her foot on the narrow little track which zigzagged up the rocky wall. Much-Afraid followed next, and then Suffering. They were on their way up Mount Injury.

# Spend Some Quiet Time

## Think About:

When the Shepherd came to her rescue at the foot of the mountain, why did He ask Much-Afraid what was wrong? Didn't He already know? Yes, He already knew, but He wanted her to tell Him. God wants us to "pour out our hearts" to Him. He wants us to learn to be honest about our feelings—then He can help us change the way we feel!

In the Bible, a man named David knew how to do this. He wrote many of the Psalms, and often he spoke about feeling "overwhelmed." He told God how he really felt and then, by the end of the psalm, he was praising the Lord! It's the same when we pour out our hearts to the Lord. It gets things out and we feel better!

## Read the Great Book:

Psalm 143:4 — My spirit is overwhelmed, and my heart is distressed.

Psalm 61:1-3 — When my heart is overwhelmed, I cry out to the Lord.

Psalm 46:1 — God heard me in the day of my trouble.

## Pray:

"Oh, Lord, when I feel as though my heart is 'overwhelmed,' help me to spend time in my 'Secret Place' with You. Help me to cry out my feelings, so they don't just stay inside me. Help me to give You my fears, doubts, and worries. Thank You for being my heavenly Daddy. Thank You for Your big, strong arms that I can run to."

Why not do this right now? Find a spot to be alone with Jesus. Imagine yourself on His lap, with His big, strong, comfy arms around you. Tell Him about any "Mount Injury"—any hurts that you have. Pour out your heart to Him and then spend some time telling Him how much you trust and love Him. You'll feel great! (And so will He.)

Once on the track, Much-Afraid discovered, to her surprise, that it wasn't nearly as hard as it had looked. It was very steep and slippery, but because she was tightly roped between Sorrow and Suffering and had the tiny bottle of the Spirit of Grace and Comfort, Much-Afraid felt quite safe.

She didn't look down unless she had to, and once when she did dare to look, she was very thankful that the Shepherd had told them to start climbing right away. Sitting on the rocks were all five of her enemies, looking up angrily. She remembered the Shepherd's warning that she would probably meet them at the top. She wondered how they would get there and realized that there must be some other way they could use.

The three steadily climbed higher and higher. They arrived at the cave just as darkness fell. Right beside the entrance was a tiny waterfall. They were thankful for a refreshing drink from its waters. Inside the cave were piles of sheepskins they could use to rest on, and Sorrow and Suffering pulled out packages of dried fruit and nuts the Shepherd had given them. They ate gratefully, then fell into a deep and peaceful sleep.

Much-Afraid woke early the next morning and walked to the entrance of the cave. She looked out to try to get a view of things from her high window. As far as the eye could see was the desert and lonely sea. The fruit orchards that they had passed through were out of sight, and everywhere she looked it was cold, empty, and sad. Even the rocky wall they were on looked even harder and more awful than she remembered.

Just then she looked up at the cliff beside the tiny waterfall. To her delighted surprise she saw a beautiful little plant. It was growing in a tiny crevice of rock and on its stem

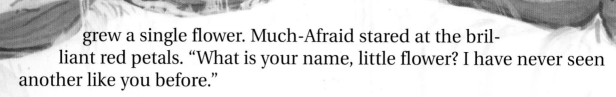

grew a single flower. Much-Afraid stared at the bril-
liant red petals. "What is your name, little flower? I have never seen another like you before."

"My name is 'Bearing-With-Love,'" the little plant seemed to whisper. "But some call me Forgiveness."

Much-Afraid realized at once that this was the new lesson the Shepherd wanted her to learn. "Why is that your name?" she asked.

A little whispering laugh seemed to pass through its leaves. "I was taken away from my family and friends and put in the prison of this rock. The ones who did this left me alone, not caring what happened to me. But I didn't stop loving, and Love helped me push through the crack. Now look at me! What flower is more blessed and satisfied than I?"

Much-Afraid looked at the flower's tiny glowing petals and wanted to be like it was. She knelt beneath the imprisoned flower and whispered, "Here I am. My name will be Bearing-With-Love too. No matter how I am hurt or mistreated, I will choose to forgive."

At that moment, a piece of rock which imprisoned the roots of the flower loosened and fell at her feet. She picked it up and gently added it to the others in her bag.

Sorrow and Suffering were waiting in the cave with a breakfast of bread, raisins, and nuts. Then the three roped themselves together again and once more began to climb Mount Injury.

After a little time they came to a place that was very steep. Suddenly Much-Afraid slipped and cut herself quite badly on the sharp rocks. It was a good thing that she

was held so tightly by the rope because her heart filled with fear and she felt like she would faint. She crouched closely to the wall and wept for fear.

Immediately Suffering came up from behind her, held Much-Afraid in her arms, and whispered, "Drink a bit from the Spirit of Grace and Comfort."

Much-Afraid trembled. "I don't even know where it is."

Suffering reached into Much-Afraid's pocket and took out the small bottle. She poured a few drops between Much-Afraid's lips and the faintness began to go away, but she still couldn't move. She drank a bit more and then felt strengthened.

They started the climb again, but it went slowly. In her fall, Much-Afraid had cut both knees so badly that she could only limp forward, moaning with pain. Her helpers were very patient, but finally Suffering asked, "What were you doing this morning at the front of the cave?"

Much-Afraid was startled by the question. "I was looking at a flower I had never seen before, growing in a rock by the waterfall."

"What kind of flower was it?" Suffering asked.

"It was the flower of Bearing-With-Love," Much-Afraid answered softly, "but some call it Forgiveness." For a few moments she was quiet, remembering the stone she had put in her bag, and the lesson she had learned from the beautiful plant. Then she said, "I

wonder if it would help if we put a few drops from the bottle on my knees?"

"That is a very good idea," said Sorrow and Suffering together. "Let's try."

As they dropped a little of the Spirit of Grace and Comfort on her knees, the bleeding stopped and the worst of the pain disappeared. Her legs were still quite stiff, and she still limped, but the three were able to move faster.

By late afternoon they reached the top of the rocky wall and came to a forest of young pine trees with moss and blueberries growing beside the path. They sat down on a mossy bank to rest and heard a voice coming toward them, singing. It was the Shepherd.

He sat beside them and cheerfully praised them for reaching the top of Mount Injury. He gently laid

His hands on Much-Afraid's wounds and immediately they disappeared. Then He began to speak to them about where this new path would lead.

"You will now go through the Forests of Danger and Tribulation." (Tribulation means big trouble.) "The path may get quite dark, and there will be storms along the way. Stay close to each other. Remember that as long as you stay on My path, nothing can really hurt you."

"The Forests of Danger and Tribulation!" Much-Afraid cried. "Oh, Shepherd, wherever will You lead me next?"

"To the next place on your journey to the High Places," He answered with a smile. "To places which will help you develop hinds' feet. Trust Me, Much-Afraid."

She looked down at her feet. They seemed more crooked than ever. Then Much-Afraid lifted her head and looked into the eyes of her Shepherd. "I will trust You to do as You have promised," she said softly. "Whatever path You lead me on, I will not fear, because You are with me."

She knelt and built another altar and added yet another stone to her bag. Then Much-Afraid started on the path which led to the Forests of Danger and Tribulation.

# Spend Some Quiet Time

## Think About:

Consider "Bearing-With-Love." When people do something wrong to us, we are to forgive them. Jesus talked about this quite a lot. In Matthew 18:22, He said to forgive 70 times 7 times! That means over and over and over again. Then He went on to tell a story about an unforgiving servant, which would be good for you to read. In Matthew 6:12, He tells us to pray that God will forgive us in exactly the same way we forgive other people. Ouch! That's a tough one.

One of the best ways I know of to get back at someone who has done something wrong to you is to think up something nice to do for them! Read Romans 12:17-21. Don't pay back evil with evil. Love those who have hurt you. Try doing something good for them.

## Memorize:

"'Be not overcome with evil, but overcome evil with good!' Romans 12:21; uh-huh, uh-huh! Romans 12:21; uh-huh!" (Say it with a rhythm!)

## Pray:

"Bearing-With-Love is a hard lesson to learn, Lord. Help! When someone does wrong to me, I want to fight back. Help me to do good to those who hurt me. Help me to be like You. You forgave the people who nailed You to the cross. You still forgive people who hurt You. You bless and help people who don't deserve it. Wow. You are really awesome. Bye for now."

# Chapter 5

## *To Full Surrender*

**M**uch-Afraid, together with Sorrow and Suffering, had crossed the desert, walked on the shores of Loneliness, and climbed Mount Injury. Now the Shepherd had told them the next part of their journey would lead them through the Forests of Danger and Tribulation.

Almost as soon as they reached the trees, they saw the mean, sickly face of Self-Pity looking out from behind one of the trunks. "Poor little Much-Afraid. Why should the Shepherd lead a lame, frightened thing like you through dangers and troubles? Really, I think this time He has gone too far."

Resentment peered out from behind another tree. "There are other ways to get to the High Places! Tell Him you won't go this way! This path is only for the strong and courageous."

Bitterness was next. "What does He think He is doing? After all you've been through, still He always has something worse ahead!"

Then Craven Fear and Pride stood on the path in front of them. "You will never make it through danger and trouble! You might as well give up and turn back."

Much-Afraid tried to keep walking, but found that she limped painfully whenever she heard their voices. Yet she couldn't put her fingers in her ears with dropping the hands of her helpers. She stopped and asked Sorrow and Suffering if they had any suggestions.

Suffering opened the little First Aid kit hanging on her belt, took out some cotton, and firmly plugged the ears of Much-Afraid. Soon her five enemies realized she couldn't hear them and became tired of bothering her. They left her alone, but planned to somehow get her attention later.

At first the forest didn't seem very bad at all. The sun was shining and Much-Afraid actually felt excited. Here she was walking through the

Forest of Danger and not really minding!

But the sun didn't shine for long. Soon huge black clouds filled the sky. Thunder rolled in the distance, and the woods became very dark and very still. Suddenly a bolt of lightning scorched across the sky, and there was a great crash as a tree fell to the earth. Then another streak of lightning flashed, and another. Soon there was thunder and lightning in every direction. The forest seemed to be groaning and shaking, and trees were falling all around them.

The strangest thing was Much-Afraid was still not really frightened. She spoke to herself words from the Great Book. "Though a thousand shall fall at your side, and ten thousand by your right hand, it will not come near to you.... for I will cover you with My feathers, and under My wings you will trust." Throughout the storm she was filled with a sense of peace as she walked between her two helpers.

At last the storm rumbled off into the distance. As they stopped to wring the water out of their clothes and hair, Craven Fear appeared and yelled at the top of his voice,

"Much-Afraid! The storm is not really gone. It will be back and it will be worse than before. Hurry back down the path and get away from these dangerous trees! There is just enough time to get away!"

"Listen," she said to her helpers, "I can't stand this any longer. Please help me, both of you!" She bent down, picked up a stone, and threw it at Craven Fear. Her two helpers actually laughed for the first time and started throwing stones toward the trees where the five enemies were hiding.

Then, just ahead of them by the path, they saw a log hut. Thunder was again rumbling closer as they hurried through the door. Suffering immediately locked the door behind them, and they were certainly glad she did!

The next minute, the five enemies were banging on the door and shouting, "Hey! Open up! The storm is starting again! You can't leave us out here!"

Much-Afraid went to the door and called through the keyhole the same words Craven Fear had spoken to her. "Hurry back down the path and get away from these dangerous trees! There is just enough time to get away!" There was a sound of angry voices outside, then hurrying feet as the storm hit in its fury.

Inside the hut, Much-Afraid and her helpers found everything they needed to stay warm and comfortable. In a short time, while the storm raged outside, the three were sitting around a crackling fire drinking hot chocolate. Much-Afraid realized with surprise that this was the happiest and most peaceful part of her journey.

As they lay down on the mattresses they found piled in a corner, she repeated to herself, softly, "He has covered me with His feathers, and under His wings I will trust."

The storm continued for several days. Much-Afraid came to know Sorrow and Suffering in a new way and began to understand more of their mountain language. She found that they were becoming more than just her helpers. They were her friends.

At last they started out once again, with their supply sack filled with water and food taken from the cabin's well-stocked pantry. The storm was over,

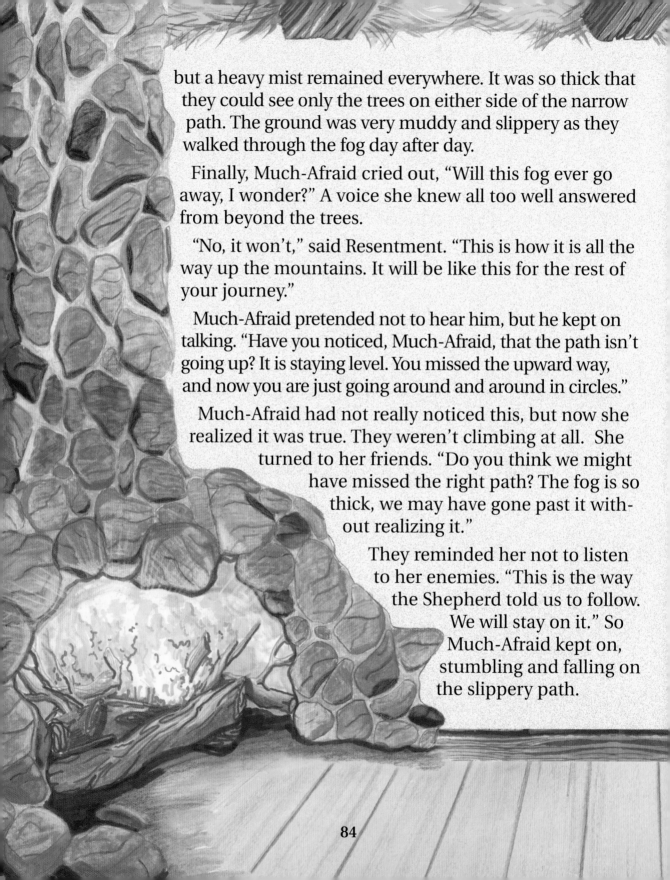

but a heavy mist remained everywhere. It was so thick that they could see only the trees on either side of the narrow path. The ground was very muddy and slippery as they walked through the fog day after day.

Finally, Much-Afraid cried out, "Will this fog ever go away, I wonder?" A voice she knew all too well answered from beyond the trees.

"No, it won't," said Resentment. "This is how it is all the way up the mountains. It will be like this for the rest of your journey."

Much-Afraid pretended not to hear him, but he kept on talking. "Have you noticed, Much-Afraid, that the path isn't going up? It is staying level. You missed the upward way, and now you are just going around and around in circles."

Much-Afraid had not really noticed this, but now she realized it was true. They weren't climbing at all. She turned to her friends. "Do you think we might have missed the right path? The fog is so thick, we may have gone past it without realizing it."

They reminded her not to listen to her enemies. "This is the way the Shepherd told us to follow. We will stay on it." So Much-Afraid kept on, stumbling and falling on the slippery path.

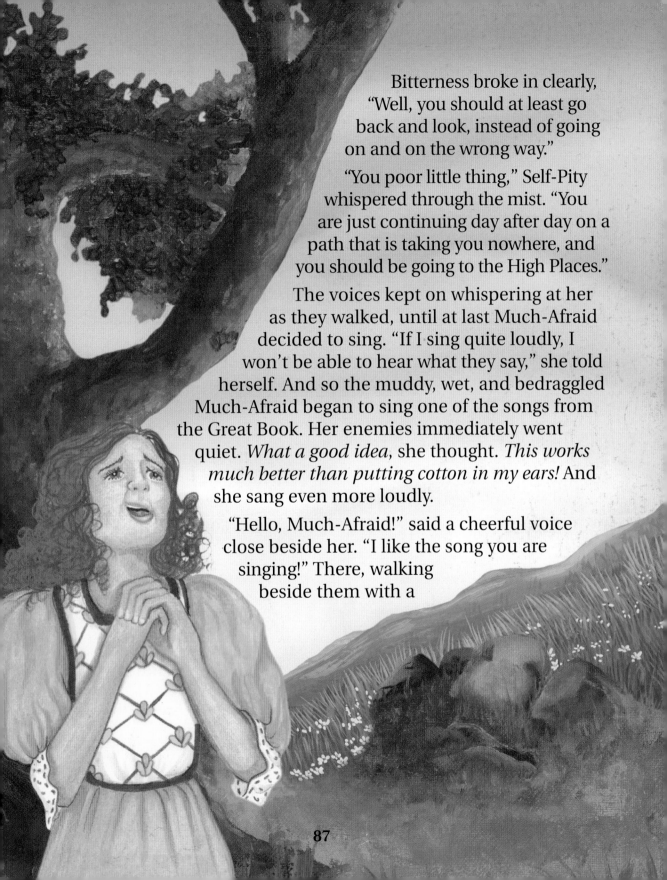

Bitterness broke in clearly, "Well, you should at least go back and look, instead of going on and on the wrong way."

"You poor little thing," Self-Pity whispered through the mist. "You are just continuing day after day on a path that is taking you nowhere, and you should be going to the High Places."

The voices kept on whispering at her as they walked, until at last Much-Afraid decided to sing. "If I sing quite loudly, I won't be able to hear what they say," she told herself. And so the muddy, wet, and bedraggled Much-Afraid began to sing one of the songs from the Great Book. Her enemies immediately went quiet. *What a good idea*, she thought. *This works much better than putting cotton in my ears!* And she sang even more loudly.

"Hello, Much-Afraid!" said a cheerful voice close beside her. "I like the song you are singing!" There, walking beside them with a

pleased smile, was the Shepherd.

Much-Afraid was very happy to see Him, but felt embarrassed by how she looked. She wondered how long He had been walking with them and how many times He had seen her slip and fall.

"Much-Afraid," He said softly, knowing her embarrasment, "I don't think of you as you are now. When I look at you, I see you as you will be when I have brought you to the Kingdom of Love. When I notice you finding the path hard, and slipping and falling, it only makes Me think of what you will be like when you are leaping and skipping on the High Places!"

Much-Afraid reached out and took His hand, and they walked on, singing the song together.

# Spend Some Quiet Time

## Think About:

How great it is to walk through the Forests of Danger and Tribulation without being afraid! God wants that for each one of us. He wants to be our peace in the middle of the storms of life. He wants to be our hiding place. He wants to "cover us with His wings."

Colossians 3:15 tells us to *let* the peace of God rule our heart. This, as with every other lesson we have learned, is a choice. We can choose to let our hearts be upset and worried, or we can choose to let God fill us with peace. Philippians 4:7 speaks of a peace that passes understanding. This idea doesn't make sense, I know. It is hard to understand, but the next time you go through danger or trouble, *let* this peace fill you.

Another powerful lesson in this part of our story is to *sing* no matter how life is treating you, and especially if Self-Pity starts speaking to you. It's very hard to feel sorry for yourself when you are praising the Lord! When you sing songs to Him, the voices of Resentment and Bitterness can't be heard anymore.

## Read the Great Book:

Psalm 36:7 — Children put their trust under God's wings!

Psalm 32:7 — God is my hiding place; songs of deliverance surround me.

Psalm 27:6 — My head is lifted above my enemies; I will sing.

## Pray:

   "Thank You for Your peace, Lord Jesus. I want it to be in my heart all day, every day. No matter what is happening—at school, in my family, with my friends—help me to choose to *let* Your peace rule. You are my hiding place. You will keep me safe in the stormy times of my life. Help me not to worry or get upset; help me to *sing* praises from my heart to You!"

   Do you know what God's very favorite song is? Throughout the Bible, He tells us to sing a "new" song (Psalm 96:1). He likes it when we sing songs we've learned at church, but He *really* likes it when we just sing to Him from our hearts how we feel about Him. He likes it when we make up tunes and sing Bible verses. Why not try it right now? Go into your Secret Place and sing unto the Lord a new song!

As she continued her journey, Much-Afraid learned many more lessons. Each time she had to lay aside what she wanted to do and decide instead to do what the Shepherd wanted. After each lesson, another stone was added to the little bag that she carried with her.

Her feet were still twisted, but Much-Afraid was hardly limping. Little by little she was changing. Her helpers seemed different too. They still held her hands, but she didn't feel any sorrow or suffering in their touch. They were becoming even better friends, and often as they walked along, all three of them sang songs from the Shepherd's Great Book.

Then came the hardest test of all. One day the path led them to a great and rocky hole. They stood carefully at the edge and peered into it. They saw nothing but darkness. It was impossible to know how deep it was, or how wide. The only sound was that of rushing waters, and Much-Afraid realized that they must be near a great waterfall.

She looked at Sorrow and Suffering and asked, "What is this place? Do you know where we are?"

They answered softly, "This is the Canyon of Full Surrender."

Much-Afraid trembled and repeated their answer, "Full Surrender." She understood immediately what that meant. She was to give up everything. She was to be willing to lay down even the Shepherd's promises. She must be willing to never receive her new name, never to have hinds' feet.

Suddenly the words of Bitterness came to her mind. "What does He think He is doing? After all you've been through, still He always has something worse ahead!"

Kneeling down at the edge of the canyon, she reached and took out the little bag of stones.

She emptied them into her lap and looked at them. "Should I throw them away?" she asked herself. "Aren't they all just empty promises? Do they really mean anything?"

One by one she picked up the stones, remembering each lesson and each time she had laid down her own desires for His. *No, I can't throw them away*, she thought. *Even if He leads me into the Canyon of Full Surrender, I will trust Him.* She put them carefully back into the little bag and stood up.

Sorrow and Suffering had been sitting quietly, watching her. Now they stood too and laughed with relief.

Much-Afraid turned to them. "What should we do?" she asked. "Can we jump across to the other side?"

"No," they said, "that would be impossible."

"Then, what are we to do?" she asked.

"We must leap down into the canyon," was their answer.

93

"Of course," said Much-Afraid. "We must leap down into the canyon."

Then for the last time on that journey (though she didn't know it at the time), she held out her hands to Sorrow and Suffering. She was weak and very tired, so instead of taking her hands, they moved closer and put their hands under her arms so she could lean on them.

Then Much-Afraid jumped into the dark Canyon of Full Surrender.

The Canyon was deep, and had she landed on the ground alone, she might have been hurt quite badly, but her friends were so strong that Much-Afraid was just a little bruised and shaken.

The Canyon was quite dark and filled with fog, so they couldn't see anything at first. They stepped forward, carefully feeling their way through the darkness. They came to a large rock that seemed to be some sort of altar. Much-Afraid spoke quietly, "This is the place. This is where I am to make an offering."

The waterfall they had heard from the head of the canyon was roaring mightily beside them. They stood in the cool shadows at the foot of the cliffs, letting the spray touch their faces. Much-Afraid listened to the thundering waters and it sounded to her like a whole orchestra playing a familiar song. Suddenly she realized it was the same music she had heard from the little river in the Valley she had called home so long ago.

*Come, oh come! Let us away*
*Lower and lower every day.*
*From the heights we leap and flow*
*To the valleys down below.*
*Always answering to the call,*
*To the lowest place of all.*

Much-Afraid watched through the dim light as the water joyfully leaped over the lip of the falls and shouted out its song. "It looks as though the waters think it is the loveliest thing in the world to be poured out like this," she said. She turned quietly to the stone altar.

This time, instead of just laying down her own desires, Much-Afraid laid her whole self on that altar. She gave her crooked feet, her twisted mouth, and her fearing heart. She gave all her hopes and dreams for ever getting to the High Places. She gave all that she was and all that she would ever be.

There came a flame from somewhere that seemed to burn deep within her heart. A beautiful sense of peace filled her and she fell asleep.

# Spend Some Quiet Time

## Think About:

What does the "Canyon of Full Surrender" mean? Sometimes children don't ever hear about this place. They hear about asking Jesus into their hearts and about going to Heaven. They hear about Jesus being their Savior.

But Jesus also wants to be *Lord*. That means Boss. That means doing what He wants, not what you want. That means obeying your parents and teachers and being nice to your brothers and sisters! That means giving your life fully to Him.

Throughout the story of Much-Afraid, we've read about "altars." An altar, in the Bible, was a place where sacrifices and offerings were made to God. In churches, an altar is a place at the front where people go to pray. Maybe you have heard someone speak about "laying your all on the altar."

Romans 12:1 tells us to "present ourselves to God a living sacrifice."

## Memorize

"Luke 6:46—Jesus said, 'Why do you call Me Lord, Lord, but you don't do the things that I say?' He wants me to hear His Word, to listen and obey!" (Say it with a rhythm.)

## Pray:

"Thank You, Jesus, for this wonderful story. Thank You that the Canyon of Full Surrender is a beautiful, peaceful place. Making You Lord and Master of my whole life is the best thing that I could ever do. Oh Jesus, be my Savior and be my Lord. Amen."

# Chapter 6

## *Hinds' Feet on High Places*

When Much-Afraid woke from a deep and peaceful sleep, there was no sign of Sorrow and Suffering. Neither was there any sign of her enemies. (They didn't want to come anywhere near the Canyon of Full Surrender.)

High above her was a cloudless sky and the peaks of the High Places, which shone dazzling white. She went to explore the Canyon and found it to be warm and quiet. The ground was a soft carpet of green grass and sweet-smelling flowers.

There was a great waterfall tumbling down into a river that was as clear as crystal. She went and dipped her fingers into the water, then stepped into one of the rocky pools. It felt so good! It was as if she was in a stream of bubbling life.

When she finally stepped out of the water and stood on the mossy bank, she happened to look down at her feet. They were beautiful! The crooked, ugly feet were gone! Then she remembered how the Shepherd had spoken of the healing streams in the High Places.

Quickly she stepped back into the pool and put her head under the clear waters and splashed them all over her face. Then she found another little pool among the rocks, still and clear as a mirror. Kneeling down, she peered into the water. The twisted mouth had disappeared! The face that looked back at her was as perfect and beautiful as that of a little child.

For three days, Much-Afraid felt as though she were wrapped in peace and happiness. She wandered around the little canyon, eating the delicious berries, bathing in the river, and resting on the mossy banks.

On the morning of the third day she woke suddenly from her sleep with a shock of joy tingling through her. Someone had called her name. She had not heard a voice, but she knew she had been called. She stood up and waited, but the only sound was the rushing waterfall.

Then it came again—tingling through her—a call ringing down from some place high above. She looked around excitedly. She felt like running up the mountains, but where was the way out of the canyon? The rocky walls were steep and straight.

Then she saw two deer like the ones she had seen that day at the foot of Mount Injury. The hart was springing up the wall of the canyon, followed closely by the hind. Much-Afraid did not wait another minute. With a flying jump she reached the edge of the wall. Then, using the same footholds as the hart and the hind, she went leaping up the cliff.

Very quickly she reached the top of the canyon, and she went on higher still toward the place that the call had come from. She leaped excitedly from rock to rock to the top of the mountain.

There was the Shepherd standing on the peak just as she knew He would be. But He wasn't dressed like a shepherd now. He was wearing a crown and royal robes, and His face shone with joy. He held out both hands and called to her with a great laugh, "You with the hinds' feet, jump over here!" She gave one last flying spring and landed beside Him on the top of the mountain.

"At last," He said, as she knelt at His feet, "at last you are here. Your night of sorrow and weeping is over, and joy comes to you in the morning. The flower of love is blooming in your heart. It is time for you to receive your new name as I promised. From now on you are Grace and Glory."

She couldn't speak, but was silent with joy and thanksgiving, and with awe and wonder. Gently the Shepherd King helped her to her feet. "Now, Grace and Glory, give me the bag of stones that you collected on your journey."

She took the bag and passed it to Him. He asked her to hold out her hands, and He emptied what was inside. She gasped with delight. Instead of the plain little stones that she had put in the bag, out fell a heap of sparking jewels!

The King took each of the precious gems and set them on a fine circlet of gold. As she watched, Grace and Glory remembered how she had almost thrown the stones away. She thought of how she almost stopped trusting His promises. She was very happy that she hadn't done either.

He placed the crown upon her head. "Now you are a daughter of the King, Grace and Glory," He said. "Now you are to live with Me here on the High Places. You will go where I go and share My work in the Valley below. I have two helpers for you."

When Grace and Glory heard those words, her eyes almost filled with tears. She remembered Sorrow and Suffering, the faithful friends He had given her before. It was through their help and gentle patience that she had been able to reach the High Places. They had gone through the same hard journey, and now she was here and they were not. She turned to the King, to beg Him to let her have them again for her helpers instead of someone new. But before she could speak, He smiled and said, "Here are the handmaidens I have chosen to be with you forever."

Two shining figures stepped forward. They wore white gowns that sparkled in the morning light. They were tall and strong and very beautiful. They came toward her with love shining from their eyes.

"Who are you?" Grace and Glory asked softly. "Will you tell me your names?"

Instead of answering, they looked at each other and smiled. Then they held out their hands as if to take hers. Grace and Glory cried out in joy, "Why, you are Sorrow and Suffering! I was longing to find you again!"

They shook their heads. "Oh, no!" they laughed. "We are no more Sorrow and Suffering than you are Much-Afraid. Don't you know that every- thing that comes to the High Places is changed? Since you brought us here, we have become Joy and Peace."

"Brought you here?" she asked. "Why, it was you two who dragged *me* here."

Again they shook their heads and smiled. "No, we could never have come here alone. Sorrow and Suffering cannot enter the Kingdom of Love, but each time you accepted us and took our hands, we began to change. Now we are to be your friends and helpers forever." They put their arms around her and hugged her tightly.

So with a new name and a glittering crown on her head, Grace and Glory came to the High Places and entered the Kingdom of Love, with Joy and Peace as her friends forever.

# Spend Some Quiet Time

## Think About:

There is so much in this short part of our story! I've listed verses below for you to look up. Think about each one as you read it. Think about Much-Afraid's journey.

Your life is like a journey. You will go through times of loneliness, trouble, and pain. You will have seasons of peace and happiness. Always walk with the Shepherd King. Trust Him to lead you on the best pathway, even though you may not understand why and where He's taking you.

One of my favorite Bible verses is Philippians 1:6: "...He who has begun a good work in you will complete it...." The Shepherd had a plan to make Much-Afraid's feet like hinds' feet, to bring her to the High Places, and to crown her with a new name. He also has a plan for your life. It is a very good plan.

## Read the Great Book:

Psalm 30:5 — Joy comes in the morning.

Esther 9:22 — Sorrow turned to joy.

Isaiah 54:11-12 — Before were storms and troubles; now there are beautiful stones.

Revelation 3:11 — Hold tightly to your crown!

2 Timothy 2:12 — If we suffer, we will also reign with Him.

## Pray:

"Lord, You see each time I lay down my own desires and do what You want...each time I learn to trust You as I walk on my path... each act of service and surrender. And You are collecting precious stones for the crown I will wear someday. Thank You for the work You are doing in my spirit-man. Thank You for changing my Much-Afraid heart into a heart that is beautiful and strong for You. Bye for now!"

The High Places where Grace and Glory and her handmaidens had entered were not the highest of all. Others towered over them up into the sky, farther than their eyes could see. Those were the Highest Places, where the King's servants went after their earthly life was over.

There were many, many other mountain ranges in every direction also. Grace and Glory gasped in awe and wonder, realizing that there was so much more to see, so much more to learn.

The King Himself trained Grace and Glory and her friends to use their hinds' feet. Instead of bounding ahead with His great strength, He carefully took only small leaps and jumps so they could keep up with Him. Grace and Glory hardly even wanted to stop to rest. Her whole life had been spent limping and struggling, and now she was leaping from rock to rock on hinds' feet!

Finally one day she was so tired that she dropped down laughing and breathless on a mossy rock. "I guess even hinds' feet need a rest now and then!" she laughed.

The King sat beside her. "Grace and Glory, do you know how I was able to make your feet like hinds' feet and set you on these High Places?"

She sat up and moved closer to Him. "How were You able to do this, my King?"

"Think back over the journey you made," He answered. "Tell Me what lessons you learned on the way."

For a long time Grace and Glory sat without speaking. She thought about the whole journey, which at times had seemed so hard, even impossible. She thought of the altars she had made along the way and of the little stones she picked up each time she laid down her own desires to follow His.

She remembered the pool in the Valley, where He had called her to follow Him to the mountains. She remembered her first meeting with Sorrow and Suffering and how she learned to let them help her. She thought of having to go down to the desert, away from the mountains, then of walking by the Sea of Loneliness. Then there were Mount Injury and the Forests of Danger and Tribulation and the days spent in the little hut during the great storm. She remembered walking through the mist and then finally arriving at the Canyon of Full Surrender.

At last she put her hand in His and said softly, "My Lord, I will tell You what I learned."

"Tell Me," He answered gently.

"First," she said, "I learned that I must accept with joy every path that You lead me on and everything that You let happen to me. I am not to try to get away from what You want for me; I am to lay down my own desires and be Your little handmaiden, Acceptance-With-Joy."

He nodded without speaking and she went on. "Then I learned that I must forgive when others are allowed to hurt me. I am to say, 'Here I am, Your little handmaiden Bearing-With-Love.' Then I will have the power to bring good out of the bad things that happen to me."

He nodded again and she smiled happily.

"The third thing I learned was that You, my Shepherd King, never looked at me as I was—weak and crooked and fearful. You saw me as I would be when You had done what You promised. You always treated me as though I were already the King's daughter and not poor little Much-Afraid." She stopped and looked up into His face. "Oh, King, I want to treat others the way You have treated me!"

He smiled at her with a very lovely smile and nodded for her to keep on.

"The fourth thing was really the first lesson I learned up here, on the High Places. Everything that happens in life, no matter how crooked and ugly it may seem to be, can be changed if I treat it with love, forgiveness, and obedience to Your will.

109

"You let us meet with the bad and wrong things that You want changed. Maybe that is why we are in this world. You want the sorrow and suffering, the ugly and wrong things, to be made into something beautiful. You want us to overcome evil with good."

At last He spoke. "You have learned well. Because of these lessons, I was able to change you from limping, crippled Much-Afraid into Grace and Glory with the hinds' feet. Now you can run and leap on the mountains.

"So remember this: As long as you are willing to be Acceptance-With-Joy and

Bearing-With-Love, you can never again become crippled, and you will be able to go where I lead. Now use your hinds' feet again. I am going to lead you to another part of the mountain."

Off He went, leaping on the mountains and skipping on the hills, with Grace and Glory following close behind. Joy and Peace went along springing beside her, and together they sang another song from the King's Great Book.

The King brought them to a beautiful, flowery meadow filled with quiet gardens and fruit trees. They spent several happy days watching the King's gardeners working carefully with the plants and vines.

One day, Grace and Glory and her friends went for a walk and found themselves on the very edge of the High Places. The great waterfall was thundering loudly beside them. From where they stood, they could see right down into the Low Places far below. There they saw a long, green valley between two chains of mountains. There was a river winding through the valley like a ribbon of light. Here and there were patches of brown and red, which seemed to be houses and villages surrounded with trees and gardens.

Suddenly, Grace and Glory knew what they were looking at. It was the Valley where she had lived for so long! She sat down on the grassy slope and remembered her home. She thought of the little white cottage where she had lived and the pastures were the shepherds cared for their flocks of sheep. In that Valley were her friends and fellow workers for the Shepherd. She thought of her neighbor, Mrs. Valiant, and smiled.

On the outside edge of the Village was the cottage where her Aunt Dismal Forebodings lived, and where she had grown up with her cousins Gloomy and Spiteful and their brother Craven Fear. She saw the homes of her other Fearing relatives, including the big old house of Lord Fearing. There was the house where Pride lived, and near it were the homes of Bitterness and Resentment, and under those dark trees lived Self-Pity.

She thought of those who had been her enemies on her journey to the High Places and of others who lived in the Valley, people who hated the Shepherd, people who refused to follow His ways. As Grace and Glory sat looking down into the Valley, her eyes filled with tears, and her heart ached with pain. "If the King can change Much-Afraid into Grace and Glory, and if Sorrow and Suffering can become Joy and Peace, surely something can be done for my Fearing relatives!" she cried.

At that very moment the King came and stood with them. Grace and Glory could hardly say her words quickly enough. "Oh, King, my relatives down there in the Valley—they are so empty and miserable! What can we do for them? They don't know anything about the High Places and the Kingdom of Love! Will You find a way to rescue them, as You rescued me?"

The King looked at her kindly, and with great happiness. He said, "I am very willing to do just that, Grace and Glory, but those unhappy people won't let Me into their homes. They don't even want Me to speak to them. I need someone to speak for Me."

"I see what You mean," she cried joyfully. "We, Joy and Peace and I, will go down and show them what You have done for us! We will tell them what You can do for them!"

"Do you think they will listen to you?" He asked, smiling gently.

"No, I don't think they will; at least, not at first," she answered. "I didn't act very nicely toward them before. But You will help me! You will teach me what to say."

Then Grace and Glory looked over at the great waterfall, which joyfully sang the water song as the waters poured themselves forth.

*Come, oh come! Let us away*

*Lower and lower every day.*

*From the heights we leap and flow*

*To the valleys far below.*

*Always answering to the call,*

*To the lowest place of all.*

Suddenly she understood. She was only one of the many, many servants of the King who had been brought to the High Places. She was only one drop among the millions of self-givers who could now pour out their lives like the waterfall. "He brought me here for this," she whispered to herself.

The King nodded. Then He began leaping and springing down the mountainside before them, choosing leaps that they could easily follow. Behind Him went Grace and Glory, with Joy and Peace beside her.

The one who had been Much-Afraid was returning to the Valley to tell everyone who would listen about the Shepherd King and what He had done for her.

# Spend Some Quiet Time

## Think About:

Remember the four lessons Grace and Glory learned. Aren't they powerful?

Several times throughout our story, we have heard about the Water Song. The lesson that Grace and Glory learned from the water is really the message of *Hinds' Feet on High Places*. King Jesus wants each one of us to fully surrender our lives to Him, and to learn to live on top of our mountains, our problems, instead of them being on top of us!

Then He wants us to pour out like the waterfall—giving and giving and giving—joyfully to other people. Read 2 Corinthians 1:4. It talks about us being able to help other people because of the way the Lord has helped us. John 7:38 also tells us that "rivers of living water" will flow out from us!

But we can't really give to others unless we live on the High Places. We need King Jesus to pour into us so we can have something to give. It is His strength, His power, His Spirit in us, that makes us able to give. Don't try to give and give to others without Him—you'll get awfully tired, and you won't get much done!

Spend time every day in your Secret Place getting filled with His love. There are people all around you who desperately need it.

## Memorize:

"Habakkuk 3, verse 19—Make my feet like hinds' feet, Lord! Let me run on the mountaintops—for You, oh Lord, will make me strong!" (Say it with a rhythm.)

(Try reading this verse from the Amplified Bible—it's great!)

## Pray:

"The world sure is in lots of trouble, Lord. People everywhere are going through really hard times. They need Your help! Help me to live on the High Places were I can better see things the way You do. Please use my life. Let me be like that waterfall. Let me pour out to others what You give to me. Help me every day to spend time with You in my Secret Place. Make my spirit-man powerful so I don't spend my life limping and struggling. I want to spend my life filled with Your strength to help others. I love You, Lord. Bye for now."

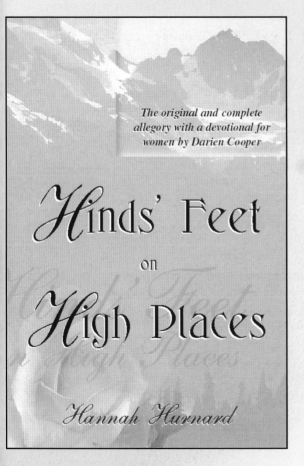

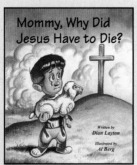

# Adventures in the Kingdom™
## by Dian Layton

### SEEKER'S GREAT ADVENTURE

Imagine an invisible Kingdom that is very, very real. It is a place where you can discover the Great King and his castle with secret towers and mysterious underground passageways. It is a place where you are invited to experience life-changing adventure!

But there is one problem...One BIG problem. Dragons.

ISBN 0-9677402-1-5

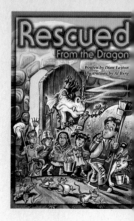

### RESCUED FROM THE DRAGON

Near the forests of Laws Forgotten, a dragon rules a village called Greed. For many years the dragon has controlled the people and told them lies about the King. The King needs someone to go to the village Greed and tell the people the truth. The King needs someone to conquer the great dragon and rescue the people. The King needs...an army!

ISBN 0-9677402-2-3

### SECRET OF THE BLUE POUCH

Seeker is about to go on a new kind of adventure and fight the greatest battle he has ever fought...but no one knows about it. No one knows what Seeker really wants. No one knows about the picture in the little white box. And no one know about the Fifteen Coins...

ISBN 0-9677402-7-4

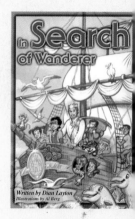

### IN SEARCH OF WANDERER

Through the window of the Secret Place Seeker and his sister, Moira, discover the truth. Their father, Wanderer, has not been seen for two years. His disappearance was a mystery. Now Seeker and his sister must do all they can to rescue Wanderer...before it's too late!

ISBN 0-9677402-8-2

### THE DREAMER

Seeker's older sister, Moira, has dreams and longings in her heart about the future. Trapper and Fantasy convince her that only in the World Beyond the Kingdom will her dreams come true. But they have lied to Moira. She doesn't realize that the path she has chosen will end in the Valley of Lost Dreams.

ISBN 0-9707919-4-1

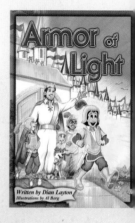

### ARMOR OF LIGHT

Through the window of the Secret Place the King shows Seeker and his friends the Land of Darkness. They see a child called NoName who is being held captive by two terribly disgusting dragons: Anger and Abuse. The King gives Seeker the Armor of Light and sends him to bring NoName...out of the Darkness and into the Light!

ISBN 0-9707919-7-6

## Available at your local Christian bookstore.

### visit www.destinyimage.com